# Introduc

The story of every character God uses
Being filled with hope allowed Abraham.
Moses willing to take on Pharaoh, and it drove the prophets to keep taking on city hall.

Jesus showered people with hope. Every crowd and every encounter revealed the spiritually and morally bankrupt: beggars, thieves, lepers, and prostitutes, all barely getting by; all wanting to see Jesus. Jesus stepped into their lives and preached forgiveness, compassion, change, and understanding. He turned bad habits and behaviors into distant memories.

As you read these reflections, you may feel so far down in the pit that no one can reach you, so overwhelmed you can't catch your breath, so broken that you wonder, "Will I ever heal? Can I ever be happy again?" But you will make it. Happiness and courage will return to your life. Jesus drops a rope down the pit. It has a big knot at its end. He's looking at you and saying, "Don't look down. Look up. Hang on. Start climbing. I'm here, right beside you!" His gentle but powerful encouragement provides the confidence to climb higher.

As you slowly but surely climb out of the pit, stay focused on Jesus. He'll be close beside you, holding your hand, helping you dodge those tugs from below. Empowered by his love and faithfulness, you will not go down there again.

When you're finally out of the pit, brush yourself off and savor the new day with refreshing opportunities written all over it. Gaze eye-to-eye at Jesus, who'll be smiling and saying, "You did it!"

It's my wish that these Advent reflections rescue you from discouragement by assuring you that Jesus is always by your side. showering you with deep, lasting hope.

---

Twenty-Third Publications, A Division of Bayard, P.O. Box 180, Mystic, CT 06355, (860) 437-3012 or (800) 321-0411, www.twentythirdpublications.com
ISBN:1-58595-528-0

Copyright ©2005 Joseph F. Sica. All rights reserved. No part of this publication may be reproduced in any manner without prior written permission of the publisher. Write to the Permissions Editor. Printed in the U.S.A.

# Lectionary Readings: Advent 2005

**First Week of Advent**
Sunday
Isaiah 63:16–17, 19; 64:2–7 • 1 Corinthians 1:3–9 • Mark 13:33–37
Monday
Isaiah 2:1–5 • Matthew 8:5–11
Tuesday
Isaiah 11:1–10 • Luke 10:21–24
Wednesday
Romans 10:9–18 • Matthew 4:18–22
Thursday
Isaiah 26:1–6 • Matthew 7:21, 24–27
Friday
Isaiah 29:17–24 • Matthew 9:27–31
Saturday
Isaiah 30:19–21, 23–26 • Matthew 9:35—10:1, 6–8

**Second Week of Advent**
Sunday
Isaiah 40:1–5, 9–11 • 2 Peter 3:8–14 • Mark 1:1–8
Monday
Isaiah 35:1–10 • Luke 15:17–26
Tuesday
Isaiah 40:1–11 • Matthew 18:12–14
Wednesday
Isaiah 40:25–31 • Matthew 18:28–30
Thursday
Genesis 3:9–15, 20 • Ephesians 1:3–6, 11–12 • Luke 1:26–38
Friday
Isaiah 48:17–19 • Matthew 11:16–19
Saturday
Sirach 48:1–4, 9–11 • Matthew 17:10–13

**Third Week of Advent**
Sunday
Isaiah 61:1–2, 10–11 • 1 Thessalonians 5:16–24 • John 1:6–8, 19–28
Monday
Zechariah 2:14–17 or Revelation 11:19; 12:1–6, 10 • Luke 1:26–38 or Luke 1:39–47
Tuesday
Zephaniah 3:1–2, 9–13 • Matthew 21:28–32
Wednesday
Isaiah 45:6–8, 18, 21–25 • Luke 7:18–23
Thursday
Isaiah 54:1–10 • Luke 7:24–30
Friday
Isaiah 56:1–3, 6–8 • John 5:33–36
Saturday
Genesis 49:2, 8–10 • Matthew 1:1–17

**Fourth Week of Advent**
Sunday
2 Samuel 7:1–5, 8–12 • Romans 16:25–27 • Luke 1:26–38
Monday
Judges 13:2–7, 24–25 • Luke 1:5–25
Tuesday
Isaiah 7:10–14 • Luke 1:26–38
Wednesday
Song of Songs 2:8–14 or Zephaniah 3:14–18 • Luke 1:39–45
Thursday
1 Samuel 1:24–28 • Luke 1:46–56
Friday
Malachi 3:1–4, 23–24 • Luke 1:57–66
Saturday
2 Samuel 7:1–5, 8–12 • Luke 1:67–79
Christmas Day
Isaiah 52:7–10 • Hebrews 1:1–6 • John 1:1–18 or 1:1–5, 9–14

## Sunday of the First Week

*Be on the alert. Mark 13:37*

# Be Alert and Available

As Betty stood on the curb waiting for the traffic light to change, she noticed a teenager standing on the opposite curb, crying. When the light changed, Betty and the girl started across the street toward each other. Just as they were about to cross paths, Betty's motherly instincts arose. Every part of her wanted to reach out and comfort that girl, but for some reason she kept walking.

Days later, the tear-filled eyes of the girl continued to haunt Betty. She said to me, "Why didn't I ask her if she needed help? Only a few seconds would have been enough to let her know that someone cared for her. Instead, I acted as if she didn't exist."

Be alert! God needs us to keep our eyes wide open so we can see those who are discouraged and help them by being a light in the dark of their night; a comforting hand on a troubled shoulder; a guide to one who is lost.

Be available! Some things just can't be put off. A child who runs to you for a hug needs one now. A timid soul who comes looking for praise needs lavish exclamations this very minute. A sad friend who requires a comforting embrace can't wait for a better time. We need to be there when we are needed, not when it's convenient for us.

Whenever we can, let's do something for others—even when we don't feel up to it; even when we have valid excuses for not making the effort. Do it. Be there. Be a shelter: a place to hide and heal, a willing, caring, available someone.

**Something to Do**
Hugging is a miracle drug. Look for overworked, overdrawn, overlooked, overwrought people and give 'em a squeeze!

**Something to Say**
*Dear Lord, help me to give to others what I need for myself. Amen.*

## Monday of the First Week

*"Lord, my servant is lying paralyzed at home." Matthew 8:6*

# Still Standing

A little boy and his mother were attending a church service, and the gregarious child couldn't sit still. The urge to stand up on the seat and look around was simply too much. His mother kept murmuring, "Sweetheart, sit down." He'd sit down for a few seconds and then get back up. She'd gently reprimand him again, "I said to sit down!"

After this happened several times, he stood up and refused to sit down. His mother put her hand on his head and gently but firmly pushed him down onto the seat. The boy sat there, smiling. Finally, he turned to his mother and said, "Mom, I may be sitting down on the outside, but I'm standing up on the inside."

When life's currents change, our real inner strength is called upon. Maybe you're facing a serious setback. You may have received a bad report from your doctor. Perhaps you're living through a broken relationship, a bankruptcy, the loss of a loved one, or some other crisis. Be alert: even when we're sitting down on the outside, we must see ourselves as standing up on the inside, filled with persistence and resilience. We must say to ourselves: "This is not going to defeat me. This is not going to steal my joy."

Jesus urges us to walk forward and experience the next opportunity waiting for us. When the dust settles, we'll still be standing strong, because we hear Jesus calling us to get up, stay up, and take one more step.

**Something to Do**
Contact a freshly hurt friend who is having difficulty getting back to normal. Offer a hug, a shoulder, or an ear.

**Something to Say**
*Dear Lord, I'll keep the faith and you'll supply the power to keep me standing. Amen.*

## Tuesday of the First Week

*"You have revealed to children." Luke 10:21*

# Become What God Believes

Two-year-old Christopher ran at top speed all over the doctor's office, unable to contain himself. When he discovered a full-length mirror, he toddled over to it, leaned forward, and gave his reflection a big smooch, an action that spoke volumes to me.

As children, we all loved to look at ourselves, totally accepting of what we saw when we looked in the mirror. As adults, it seems that on some mornings, when we stand before a mirror and ask, "Mirror, mirror on the wall, who's the fairest of them all?" the mirror says, "Step aside, so I can see who's behind you!"

For many of us, the self-accepting child Jesus invites us all to be is still within us, but covered with layers of self-doubt and feelings of inadequacy. These layers have accumulated from listening too long to people tell us we aren't good enough, pretty enough, or smart enough. The result is that we no longer like the person we see in the mirror; we've lost the small child's self-assurance.

Stop allowing other people to play games with your mind. Don't let them deceive you into thinking that your value has diminished. Start agreeing with God, determined to be the unique person God made. Valuable. One of a kind. Irreplaceable. How we see ourselves and how we feel about ourselves will have a tremendous impact on how far we go in life.

### Something to Do
Write a thank-you note to someone who has been a positive influence in your life. Oh, and look in the mirror (before you're made up or dressed up) and smile. Do it every day.

### Something to Say
*Dear Lord, help me to see myself as you see me. Amen.*

# Wednesday of the First Week

*Immediately they left their nets and followed him. Matthew 4:19–20*

# Reach Out and Warm a Heart

Louis, a boy who was popular with the other kids in his class, was diagnosed with leukemia. He remained strong throughout his treatment, joking and playing games with the many friends who came to visit him. When Louis lost his hair to chemotherapy, all the boys in his sixth-grade class welcomed him back to school by shaving their heads.

We all need encouragement. When love walks out the door, when a friend moves out of town, when the job ends, or the bank fails, God seems distant. Prayer fades in our throats before we utter a word. We all need someone to believe in us, to reassure and reinforce us, to lift up the wounded, calm the fearful, and soothe the frantic child within each of us. We need each other's warmth to survive the winters of our lives, to help us pick up the pieces and go on, even if that encouragement takes the form of a shaved head.

Jesus issues an incredible directive—follow me. What soothing words for the lonely to hear! So many people of all ages are out there, aching for someone to put an arm around them and squeeze tightly. People's ears are hungry for something positive, encouraging, and refreshing to the spirit.

Jesus delights in small, spontaneous acts of encouragement—a prayer, a hug, or a touch on the shoulder.

## Something to Do
Think of someone who might need a hug. Show this person that you care. Write the letter. Make the phone call. Visit the neighbor you've been meaning to see. Your small act of kindness might make someone's day.

## Something to Say
*Dear Lord, someone I'll meet today is lonely and afraid. Give me your words to bring that person comfort, courage, or calm. Amen.*

## Thursday of the First Week

*"Everyone who hears these words builds their house on rock."* Matthew 7:24

# Words Too Seldom Heard

Do you ever have difficulty expressing your feelings? You're not alone. Take, for example, those two seldom-heard but highly effective words: "I'm sorry." The words "I'm sorry" don't need to assign blame to one side or another. For many of us, however, saying "I'm sorry" is a painful admission of fault—as if saying these two simple words reveals some weakness or vulnerability within us.

Yet being vulnerable, being able to say, "I was wrong," is one of the surest signs of strength within our relationships and ourselves. Our ability to apologize announces that we are sensitive to the pain and moods of others. The magic words "I'm sorry" have unlimited power to heal and restore.

We also struggle with the words, "I love you." Why is it so difficult for some people to say these three simple words? Why do we leave this phrase behind, regarding it as a remnant of our earlier, more romantic selves? Have we come to believe that after a time, love speaks for itself, that the words "I love you" are implied in a relationship?

As relationships and the people in them inevitably change, it's important we reaffirm that some things are constant. "I'm sorry" and "I love you" are powerful foundational reinforcements. Don't use these words sparingly!

**Something to Do**
Who in your life needs to hear some seldom-heard words? Even a simple "Hello, how are you doing?" can brighten someone's day.

**Something to Say**
*Dear Lord, thank you for the love you give me through my family, friends, and other people in my life. Amen.*

## Friday of the First Week

*And their eyes were open.* Matthew 9:30

# How We Once Were

How long since you did some fun, childlike things—like jumping into a pile of leaves? Or gathering armfuls of lilacs and bringing them to friends so their homes would smell like spring? Or going up the down escalator? Let's take off that mask of adulthood and be children again. By doing so, we can tap into a boundless fountain of youth within ourselves.

We can't always escape the bad times in life—there's suffering, sorrow, and pain—but we can decide to give ourselves a hurt-break day. On this day, engage in a few childlike activities. No matter how down or rotten you feel, try smiling at yourself in every mirror you pass. First thing in the morning. Last thing at night.

Do fun things just because you want to be impulsive and adventurous. Listen to the long-lost child inside you and catch the simple blessings that often go unnoticed. Look for ways to enjoy life's small pleasures. A pat on the back. A full moon. An empty parking space. A crackling fire. A great meal. A glorious sunset. Go to a park and feed the ducks. Drink hot chocolate with marshmallows and whipped cream.

At the end of your hurt-break day, congratulate yourself. Pick up the phone and share some special thought with a caring friend. Enjoy life's tiny delights. There are plenty for all of us.

### Something to Do
Make the first day of every month a hurt-break day for yourself. Open only mail that is good (no bills). Do something that you really enjoy.

### Something to Say
*Dear Lord, how great it is, the way you make children the treasures they are. May I always learn from them. Amen.*

## Saturday of the First Week

*Freely you received, freely give.* Matthew 10:8

# Ready? Set? Give!

Maria felt utterly helpless. She didn't know what to do or say as she listened to her friend, Patricia, whose husband had just walked out on her for a younger woman.

The next morning, Maria went to see Patricia. As they sat talking over coffee, the doorbell rang. A neighbor arrived with a dust rag and furniture polish. She quietly went to work, tackling a chore Patricia hated. She prayed for Patricia while dusting the furniture. As Maria continued listening to her friend grieve, the phone rang several times with calls from friends, all expressing their concern.

Too often, we mouth the cliché, "If there's anything I can do, just let me know." Instead of phoning in your offer of help, get up, go out, and give generously. Stop trying to figure out what everybody else can do for you, and start propping up others who are feeling down, drained, and discouraged.

Buy someone a cup of coffee tomorrow morning and say, "Do you need to talk?" Mow someone's lawn, pull some weeds, shovel snow, or wash a few windows. Make a cake, then knock on a door and ask, "Need some company?" Go to the hospital and cheer someone up.

We can never untangle all the woes in other people's lives. We can't produce miracles overnight. We can bring a cup of cold water to a thirsty soul or a scoop of laughter to a lonely heart. Keep looking for ways to help others.

**Something to Do**
Think of someone you know who is hurting and come up with actual ways you can reflect God's love to them.

**Something to Say**
*Dear Lord, never let me miss an opportunity to help a friend who has been hit with bad news. Amen.*

## Sunday of the Second Week

*"Prepare the way of the Lord, clear a straight path."* Mark 1:3

# Soul Survivor

Many of us have learned that we can achieve happy, healthy, and whole lives by first turning inside and giving ourselves a good soul clean-up. Here I refer to the soul as the sum total of our dreams, thoughts, feelings, beliefs, values, decisions, and commitments: components that absolutely define each of us as a unique child of God. It's the real, genuine, and authentic person inside created uniquely in the image and likeness of a loving God. Soul is the safe harbor where we go to hear God's healing, encouraging voice speak to us during the difficult and joyful times of life.

Soul clean-up is good spiritual practice in preparing us to welcome Jesus. It enables and encourages us to unclog and sweep away all the things we don't love. We can get rid of everything that's had a non-productive and unhealthy impact on us: unpleasant memories, overly critical people, imagined worries, false fears, and defeating experiences. All leaving us feeling afraid, anxious, rushed, upset, trapped, pinned down, and drained.

Once the soul's unblocked, we'll have the wisdom to discern and decide which battles we are going to fight while keeping for ourselves the power to run our lives. We will accept today as a gift and make the most of it.

**Something to Do**
Write down a list of stuff you want to clean out of your soul. Next to each item, write how you'll sweep it out of your life. For example, if panic paralyzes your soul, choose to pause, catch your breath, remain calm, and then respond.

**Something to Say**
*Dear Lord, help me get rid of all the rubbish that keeps me from hearing your voice speak to me. Amen.*

## Monday of the Second Week

*Your sins are forgiven. Rise and walk.* Luke 5:23

# Let 'Em Have It!

I stopped briefly to watch two boys quarreling. Their dialogue went like this: "You're stupid!" "Well, so are you." "Not as stupid as you!" "Yeah? That's what you think." They soon finished their exchange and went their separate ways. When I returned a few minutes later, the boys were playing again, having forgotten the whole thing.

Grown-ups usually don't have such a quick, kiss-and-make-up response. Adults develop razor-sharp memories of past wrongs and carry them around, ready at a moment's notice to use them as ammunition. Every time you think of something in your past that has caused you great pain, you stand at a fork in the road. And each time, you must choose which road you're going to take: Carry It Circle or Bury It Boulevard.

Carry It Circle. You're lugging around unforgiveness and just can't seem to let it go. Instead, you stumble along, going in circles, living according to the script of painful past experiences.

Bury It Boulevard. The second road leads to a special graveyard where you can bundle up and bury all your pain and bitterness through forgiveness. You can finally free yourself from the desire to get even, the deep yearning to "let 'em have it, let 'em rot" syndrome.

You must make up your mind which road you'll take to release and totally forgive everyone who's ever done you any wrong. It's the only way to break the endless cycle of resentment and retaliation.

**Something to Do**
If you're carrying around unforgiveness, try writing these words on a piece of paper: "I forgive (person's name)." Speak these words over and over. Don't stop until you get the message.

**Something to Say**
*Dear Lord, after I bury my painful past, please give me long-term amnesia. Amen.*

## Tuesday of the Second Week

*"A man has a hundred sheep...."* Matthew 18:12

# What's the Rush?

Some time ago a newspaper in Tacoma, Washington carried the story of Tattoo, the basset hound. In a hurry, Tattoo's owner accidentally shut the dog's leash in the car door and took off. Police officer Terry Filbert spotted the passing vehicle with something dragging behind it: Tattoo. Officer Filbert chased the car to a stop, and Tattoo was rescued before he came to harm.

There's too much Tattoo-like behavior going on—hurry sickness! We spend our days going from one task to another, haunted by the fear that there are not enough hours in the day to do what needs to be done. Hurry sickness weighs us down with the burden of all the things we've failed to say no to, plus forgetting important dates, missing appointments, and not following through. We're left feeling tired, drained, angry, and frustrated. What's the solution?

We can become unhurried people through the daily practice of slowing down. Slowing down involves choosing to place ourselves in positions where we have to wait. During Advent, why not drive in the slow lane on the expressway? Instead of trying to pass, say a prayer as others whiz by. Put the horn under a vow of silence. Eat your food slowly. Go one day without wearing a watch. And when you're at a grocery store, get in the longest check-out lane.

The list can go on. We must find ways to deliberately choose waiting, ways that make hurry impossible. We can survive without hurry. Practice enough and we will become unhurried people.

**Something to Do**
At the end of the day, go over the day's events with Jesus. See what he's saying to you through them, and then hand any anxieties or regrets over to him.

**Something to Say**
*Dear Lord, slow me down. Amen.*

## Wednesday of the Second Week

*"Come to me and I will give you rest."* Matthew 11:28

# Struck by an Arrow of Adversity

My friend Theresa's life is a litany of heartaches. Her husband had a massive heart attack while playing blackjack at a casino. After his death, she discovered piles of debt he'd built up from maxing out credit cards and re-mortgaging their home. Foreclosure followed. Her son sits in a Florida jail after committing armed robbery and murder. Her daughter is high most of the time and appears regularly at the hospital emergency room when she overdoses.

When Theresa shared her experiences with our prayer group, she described feeling as if she were being struck by arrows that plunged deeply. "But my life's arrows were only momentary setbacks," she added. "I decided rather than dwelling on my hurts, I'm dumping them in Jesus' lap. Rather than allow myself to re-live them, I'm releasing them to Jesus."

Which arrow has struck you recently? Physical pain? Unfair treatment? False accusations? Betrayal? Struggles at home? While I have no magic formulas for making the arrows go away, let me suggest using a page from Theresa's life for your healing. Instead of wallowing in self-pity, wondering "Why me?" turn you pain over to Jesus. Dump all the pieces in his lap. Next, let it go. Look around and see the faces of those who will bring you healing, patience, and comfort even when you're convinced you can't survive another day.

Finally, start your walk in the land of beginning again.

### Something to Do
Take a paper bag, write "Jesus" on it, and tape it up high on the back of a door in your home. Whenever you pray about one of life's arrows, write it down on a piece of paper. Place it in the paper bag. Leave all the arrows there and get on with your life.

### Something to Say
*Dear Lord, I will place my troubles in your lap and let them go. Amen.*

## Thursday of the Second Week

*"Hail, favored one! The Lord is with you."* Luke 1:28

# I Need Only Be Me

Singer-actress Judy Garland said, "Always be a first-rate version of yourself, instead of a second-rate version of somebody else." This quote carries with it a time-honored moral: you have a right to be yourself.

People try to make us into what they want us to be. And after a while, we give up and make ourselves over in order to be accepted and loved. We create disguises and hide behind them. Yet the person we're attempting to cover up, just to fit in, is precisely the person those who love us are seeking.

Each of us arrived in the world with a face like none other, a voice that brought a brand new sound, and a mind that would be entirely unique. Find a healthy atmosphere in which to grow and discover this distinctiveness. There are people who will take the time to see your unique spark and help you develop your special abilities. We recognize and appreciate this when we say things like, "I can be myself around her," or "He likes me for who I am." Enjoy being in a space where there's nothing to hide.

Be sure of this: we are favored, privileged, and precious in God's eyes. But with privilege comes responsibility. We mustn't let anyone tell us who we are. If we do this, it shows we care little for ourselves, and we end up as someone's doormat. The real you is far better than anything you or others can concoct.

### Something to Do
The next time you pass a mirror, look in and say, "You know it's true. There's only one you!"

### Something to Say
*Dear Lord, thanks for loving me just the way I am. I am blessed. Amen.*

## Friday of the Second Week

*"Look, he is a glutton and a drunk."* Matthew 11:19

# Give the Weeds a Break

I've never forgotten what Andrea said to her husband, "If I'm so bad, why did you marry me?" There's little that's more destructive and demeaning than the casual put down, and he regularly used her as the object of his degrading humor.

When we use put downs we treat people more like weeds than the flowers they truly are. Speaking of a simple weed, Emerson called it "a plant whose virtues have not yet been discovered." How many people have we written off as weeds because, for some lame reason, they appeared unworthy of our love and attention?

In our efforts to fit people into convenient categories, we end up minimizing their worth or excluding them without reason. We use age, sex, social standing, monetary status, color, religion, nationality—any number of things to distance ourselves from those who are different. This saves us the trouble of thinking independently and experiencing each individual as a distinct, deserving person.

We'll find no shortage of put downs directed at us. If we allow them to continue, we relinquish our self-worth. We need to stand up for ourselves like Andrea did, and say these words: I have value.

Most people we meet are probably worthy of more consideration than we give them. We may be surprised to find that they're not weeds after all, but rather flowers we've failed to appreciate.

### Something to Do

If you tend to put people down, try this: find a rubber band. Put it on your wrist, where it is to remain for the rest of Advent. Now listen very closely to the way you talk about people or to people. Every time you hear yourself putting down someone, snap that rubber band on your wrist to condition yourself to stop the put downs.

### Something to Say

*Dear Lord, may my words lift people rather than level them. Amen.*

## Saturday of the Second Week

*"I tell you Elijah has already come, and they did not recognize him."* Matthew 17:12

# Wrap Your Arms Around Hope

Dusk darkened the Sistine Chapel as a weary, doubtful Michelangelo climbed down the ladder from his scaffolding. He'd been lying on his back since dawn, painting the ceiling. After eating a lonely dinner, he wrote a sonnet to his aching body. The last line: "I'm no painter."

When the sun shone again, Michelangelo arose from his bed, climbed up onto the scaffold, and labored another day on his magnificent vision of the Creator.

What pushed him up the ladder? Hope!

Sometimes we're blindsided by life-shattering problems. We can't push difficult situations back, but we can rise to their challenges, because we are hope huggers. Life's setbacks can leave us disgusted and discouraged. But hope huggers don't bail out or run away. When the going gets tough, they hang in with perseverance.

"After experiencing a difficult breakup, I was one step away from crippling fear," Louis admitted. "I was reluctant to walk through another door. I hesitated, but eventually took the step over the threshold, knowing Jesus was inside urging, 'Come forward.' It's hard; it's a trust-investment, leading to new growth-possibilities."

No matter what we're going through, it's not here to stay. It will pass. The mending process takes time. We're on a journey of becoming whole again. Keep hugging hope and looking for the doors ahead.

**Something to Do**
Create a hope-reminder card to keep in your purse or wallet. Refer to it often. (Consider copying Isaiah 40:31 or 1 Peter 1:3 onto it.)

**Something to Say**
*Dear Lord, no matter what happens, I'm hugging hope. Amen.*

### Sunday of the Third Week

*"I'm not the Messiah, but the voice of one making the path straight."* John 1:20, 23

# Shall We Dance?

Tammy constantly agonized over the future of her relationships. Her endless need for reassurance meant that she was always full of anxiety. Finally, she asked me for help. Together we determined that this continual uncertainty pushed people away. Tammy decided to relax and enjoy what was happening to her moment by moment.

If you've become trapped in feelings of discomfort, disappointment, and dissatisfaction, it's time to learn new dance steps: those of happiness and wholeness. Try these three simple steps:

1. Face it. Look the problem squarely in the face. Don't quietly bury it deep down inside your heart and mind and hope it goes away. When we do that, one day the problem will re-appear in our lives and cause more pain than we're able to handle.

2. Trace it. Get to the root of the problem by asking, "Why am I so angry? Why can't I get along with people? Why am I always so negative?" Look deeply within and find the origin. Only then can you deal with the problem and begin to change.

3. Replace it. Once we've recognized why and how we're hurting ourselves, we can choose to stop. Find healthy alternatives—patience, forgiveness, and trust—to replace old thinking, so you're not likely to revert to old patterns.

The new dance steps may initially cause anxiety. But change is better than standing still, and most change is for the better.

**Something to Do**
Choose a partner—a trusted friend, spiritual director, counselor, or parish priest and dance through these three steps together.

**Something to Say**
*Dear Lord, with every step I take today to change, I'll leave more of my problems behind. Amen.*

## Monday of the Third Week

*"She was greatly troubled at what was said and wondered about its meaning." Luke 1:29*

# One Mouth and Two Ears

One of my students battled severe depression and tried to communicate this to her parents. More than once she spoke to them of her world caving in around her, and her parents—for whatever reason—chose not to hear. She even went so far as to tell them that she had considered suicide. Still her parents didn't listen. When she finally did attempt suicide—and fortunately failed—her parents were dumbstruck. Can you imagine this young woman's frustration when they said, "Why didn't you tell us you were having problems?"

My favorite motto is: "Nobody cares how much you know unless they know how much you care." Talking is sharing; listening is caring. The very best in us is brought out when we listen to others. We've all experienced the distress of talking with people who are so self-absorbed that they don't hear a word we say—all the while preparing their own dazzling comments. Perhaps Diogenes, over two thousand years ago, had such people in mind when he said, "We have two ears and only one tongue in order that we may listen more and speak less."

When someone says, "Can we talk?" it's time to turn off the cell phone, television, or computer and face that person eyeball to eyeball. And if you want to talk, wait for your turn. Each day a new person sits across from us waiting to be discovered by anyone who'll take the time to listen.

### Something to Do
Give a gift to your spouse, parent, or child that can still be used after Christmas: a listening ear—and heart.

### Something to Say
*Dear Lord, help me curb the urge to give advice when I have only been asked to listen. Amen.*

## Tuesday of the Third Week

*"Even after you saw it, you did not change your minds...."* Matthew 21:32

# Time for a Change

My friend's wife always wanted to visit her relatives in Poland, the country of her parents' birth. Though they could certainly afford to go, my friend thought it was a frivolous way to spend money. There was always a less expensive place to go, car and house payments, or the need for a snow blower, or the children's college education.

Today, the house and car are paid in full, he has his new snow blower, and the children are educated and married. But his wife never realized her dream. She died last year. It pains me to hear him say, "I wish I had…" as we so often do in hindsight.

How many possibilities have we missed because we've waited for a more convenient moment? How many people have we failed to celebrate because we thought we'd have forever? I was raised to work hard, save money, and invest in the future. By doing these things, we're told, someday we'll be able to enjoy what we dream about. The sad part is that, too often, by the time we reach those golden years, we no longer need the same things. Or we're too tired, too ill, or too set in our ways to enjoy them.

Avoid putting things off and making excuses. Today is waiting to be experienced and enjoyed. Only with DINsight (Do-It-Now sight) can we see what's waiting for us. Alan recently said, "Since I've had cancer, my wife and I have forgotten the meaning of tomorrow. When one of us says, 'Let's…' the other says 'Yes!' before the sentence is finished. Cancer has improved my sight."

### Something to Do
Turn off voice mail, phone, TV, Palm Pilot, and computer. Give yourself time to see and delight in today's pleasures and people.

### Something to Say
*Dear Lord, seeing today's blessings makes me step back and say, "Ahhh!" Amen.*

## Wednesday of the Third Week

*". . . the blind recover their sight, the lame walk, and the deaf hear."* Luke 7:22

# Brighten Up

We all have disturbing, disrupting periods of failure, sadness, loss, trouble, frustration, and trial. When terrible things happen, some people become stuck in a dark valley. Others refuse to let the tragedy hold them down, and find a sense of purpose in their lives and the strength to go on. How? By cuddling up to the light.

Utilizing the acronym LIGHT, we can map out a step-by-step plan to bring us out of our dark valleys:

• *Learn.* We can learn much from whatever pain or problem, hurt or hassle has us temporarily living in darkness. We begin to see that spiritual values are more than just theories: they brighten our way.

• *Insight.* Fresh thoughts begin to flow, and new ways to adapt come to light. Now our eyes are open to options overlooked, possibilities pushed aside, changes crushed, and suggestions ignored.

• *Guide.* Let God guide us to a place to cry, someone to care, and the security of intimate friends who will share our hurt so our stay in the dark valley is not prolonged.

• *Heave* your darkness out the window, and let the light shine in.

• *Trust.* As we keeping moving toward daylight, we trust we're not alone. God enters our dark valleys and makes them less painful. Less frightening.

**Something to Do**
Create brighten-up cards, using 3" x 5" index cards. On the front, write out Philippians 4:8. Tape a birthday candle to the back. Mail to those you know who are stuck in a dark valley.

**Something to Say**
*Dear Lord, your light is waiting just around the corner for me to embrace it. Amen.*

## Thursday of the Third Week

*"What did you go out to the desert to see?"* Luke 7:24

# Cut the Rope

When I was a first-year high school religion teacher, I soon stopped going to the teachers' lounge. Worse than the haze of cigarette smoke that constantly hung over the room was the cloud of emotional negativity. "Can you believe what they want us to do for spirit day?" "I got that Smith kid again this year in math. He's a loser." So it went, a constant stream of criticism and negative comments.

I soon discovered a group of teachers in the athletic office. They were positive and believed they could handle anything that was thrown at them. I hung out with them and learned to appreciate that every student arrives at school with a unique story.

There are two types of people: anchors and motors. Anchor people always spread negative rumors, find fault with everyone and everything, and pollute the air with judgment, complaints, and blame. Anchors drag us down with their negative attitudes. Motor people are the opposite. They are positive, nourishing, and uplifting. They believe in us and encourage us to go after our dreams and learn from our mistakes. They keep us moving along.

Jesus faced off with anchor people who kept track of other people's mess-ups. They loved to resurrect them and recite them whenever they had a chance. But Jesus wouldn't allow anchor people to pull others down. Instead, he looked at everyone with compassion and care, seeing their inner beauty and worth as God's children.

Let's lose the anchors and run with the motors before we sink.

**Something to Do**
Make a concerted effort to free yourself from anchor people. If that's impossible, then dramatically decrease the amount of time you spend with them.

**Something to Say**
*Dear Lord, help me to be a life-lifter and not a life-sinker. Amen.*

## Friday of the Third Week

*"He was a burning and shining lamp and you rejoiced in his light."* John 5:35

# Please Release Me!

Cindy couldn't wait to get home and tell her father that she was to be a star in the school Christmas play. Thrilled, he asked if she would be Mary. "No, Daddy, I'm going to be a star!" "You mean an angel?" "Daddy," she exclaimed, "I'm a star. I lead people to Jesus."

Star people work to overcome repetitive, self-destructive obstacles. But others still want to cling to whatever it is that's paralyzing their growth. We crave release, but refuse to release. We risk sabotaging our best plans, our most inspired ideas, and our relationships with others.

But star people listen to the inner urging that says, "Let go. Be free," by practicing the four Rs:

- *Recognize* that many of the biggest obstacles we have to overcome are ones that we spend time and effort constructing.
- *Remedies* will be needed to replace loneliness, hopelessness, isolation, boredom, and health consequences. What matters most now is how we go about healing and helping ourselves.
- *Resolve* to see life as a series of new moments and not a stagnant reflection of our past.
- *Release* is the final step. Star people don't see release as a triumph, but as something awesome and wonderful.

We can make ourselves better, a little bit at a time. We can stop being the stumbling block in our own path to happiness.

**Something to Do**
Name some of the obstacles that are holding you back right now. Take time this week to apply the four Rs to at leat one of these, as you prepare your heart and mind to receive the child Jesus.

**Something to Say**
*Dear Lord, thank you for putting star people in my life to lead me through my obstacle courses. Amen.*

## Saturday of Third Week

*"Judah became the father of Perez and Zerah, whose mother was Tamar."* Matthew 1:3

# Pruning the Family Tree

When we dig into Jesus' family tree we find all kinds of skeletons in his closet. Remember Tamar (Genesis 38:6)? Judah's promise to Tamar was forgotten—or ignored. But Tamar refused to be forgotten. She does the unthinkable. If her father-in-law wouldn't give her his son, Shelah, so she could produce an heir for her dead husband, she'd see to it that she had that heir. She disguised herself as a prostitute and seduced Judah. Nine months later, as a result of this union, she bore twins. One of them, Perez, is listed in the messianic line. Tamar is often a forgotten woman because her story isn't pretty and we'd rather overlook it. But God didn't overlook Tamar. She's the first woman listed in the genealogy of Jesus.

The message of Jesus' family is this: God sees the best in everybody. We must resist jumping on the bandwagon with people who are hard, critical, and judgmental toward others. If we look hard enough and long enough, we can find something positive in every person we know, even our worst enemy.

Stop thinking that God won't accept us as we are. Not only does God accept us, but he forgives our sins, changes our hearts, and uses us to bring good news in this world. Just as God used Tamar.

### Something to Do
Snow fences don't stop snow, but rather channel drifts out of roads and homes. Build a "snow fence" by wiring five large tongue depressors together (one for each person who always sees the best in you). Reflect on how each person finds something positive in you.

### Something to Say
*Dear Lord, you always give me room to grow and become better. Amen.*

## Sunday of the Fourth Week

*"How can this be? May it be done to me according to your word."* Luke 1:34, 38

# The One Essential Ingredient

Have you ever wondered how Mary felt when Gabriel told her she was going to have a baby? Surely she had some reservations. Her thoughts may have run the gamut from "Are you kidding?" to "No way. It can't be," to "I'm going to be in big trouble when Joseph hears about it," to "I'll be the talk of Nazareth." Mary was a real person who had to live her life one day at a time. She didn't get sneak previews of how everything would turn out. Yet she faced the situation with the willingness to trust God for the outcome.

When life seems out of control, we need to trust God in every situation—even when we don't understand it. Too often we trust God only when we've gotten our own way. When we prayed but didn't get what we wanted, or we didn't get the answer we were looking for, God may have been saying "It's not the right time. You're not ready for that. I have something better in mind for you."

We may not be in a very good place right now, and we're wondering, "Will it ever get better?" Let's bring it to God and look beyond where we are. Let's pray and listen—and be ready to accept the answer. Trust God by believing he knows what's best for us. How? It's kind of like falling. When we fully trust someone, we can fall backward toward that person, confident that we'll be okay.

**Something to Do**
Invite friends over. Take turns going on a trust walk: where one person is blindfolded and led around by others. Talk about this experience, then read Jeremiah 1 and examine Jeremiah's trust relationship with God.

**Something to Say**
*Dear Lord, you are a God of dreams and not disappointments. I trust you to know what is best for me. Amen.*

## Monday of the Fourth Week

*"Do not be afraid, Zechariah, because your prayer has been heard."* Luke 1:13

# Prayer as Ointment

For the most part, life is anything but easy. It's like eating an ice cream cone on a hot summer day—just when we think we have it licked, it drips all over us. But think about this: "Blessed are the flexible, for they shall not be bent out of shape." Prayer is the ointment that keeps our spirits flexible in the hands of God.

Use this ointment before bedtime to drain all the negative emotions out of your life. To live a wholesome life it's necessary to drain fear, suspicion, hatred, bitterness, resentment, envy, jealousy, and self-pity from our souls. Let's pray that Jesus will fill us with the healthy emotions of hope, humor, courage, cheer, enthusiasm, and self-confidence. Use this ointment to sustain yourself, to hold on and never quit in life.

How I love these words scratched on a basement wall alongside the Star of David. Etched by a nameless German Jew in hiding, they were discovered after the end of World War II:

I believe in the sun even when it's not shining.
I believe in love even when I don't feel it.
I believe in God even when he is distant.

This person knew the sustaining power of prayer. Even in dreadful darkness, this person basked in the warm sunlight of God's presence through prayer.

Tell God what you need. Keep praying. Every day. God is waiting to hear from us.

**Something to Do**
If you were trapped in a basement, what would you scratch on the wall?

**Something to Say**
*Dear Lord, you are the hero of my soul. I love to talk with you in prayer. Amen.*

## Tuesday of the Fourth Week

*"Don't be afraid, Mary. You have found favor with God."* Luke 1:30

# Opportuniy Knocks

Why do we so often freeze up on the threshold of a God-given opportunity? Simple: flimsy faith and a faulty view of God. Flimsy faith looks to God as the parent in the sky who'll get us out of trouble and solve our problems. But fervent faith challenges us to face reality, confront our fears, and act to solve our problems, while praying to God for courage and the strength to go forward.

Fervent faith gives us the power to act with persistence and perseverance. When we seize opportunities, our faith has the ability to light up another person's life. It happens when a son goes to visit his elderly parents after work. He helps them with the shopping, bills, and medications. He listens to their repetitious stories with respect.

Fervent faith is when parents hang in there and refuse to give up on their teenage son or daughter, no matter how painful it is. Fervent faith is when people stand by a friend who has cancer, even when they're afraid.

Mary trusted God. She somehow knew that if she crumbled with flimsy faith, this God-given opportunity would pass her by. Mary's fervent faith, together with her fine view of God, turns her fear around so she isn't stopped from doing what God called her to do.

Don't allow flimsy faith to let you collapse. Be a person who not only sees God's opportunities, but one who charges through them with fervent faith.

**Something to Do**
What beautiful opportunities is God seeking to bring to your attention? Be still for a moment. Then write them down and try to do them—even if they seem impossible.

**Something to Say**
*Dear Lord, when you give me an opportunity, I'm going to say, "Yes!" Amen.*

## Wednesday of the Fourth Week

*"...the infant in my womb leaped for joy."* Luke 1:44

# Don't Let the Joy Meter Run Out

Sometimes life can get us down, can't it? At times like these we could stand a little joy. It's within our grasp once we toss out the joy-deflators who enjoy dumping depressing thoughts into our heads, thoughts that leave us downcast and defeated.

Joy deflators have a negative impact on our lives as they continually conjure up all the "Woe is me" stories while repeating, "Life is miserable, boring, depressing, unfair, confusing, and cruel." Each day seems to be a test of endurance rather than an exciting adventure. Their melancholy spin is a guarantee for instant misery.

It's time to be our own spin doctors and focus intently on the basic rule of joy inflators: "Outlook determines outcome. As we think, so we feel." It's time to surround ourselves with joy inflators and listen to their cheerful spin: "There's good in every person and it's up to us to bring it out."

Moments of joy touch to us more deeply than our problems. On the darkest days, we don't give up or hang back. God is near. Look around, and move forward with hope-filled joy. From our joy we draw the courage and strength to face the harshest extremes and the cruelest of fates. Even with broken bones, our spirit of joy expands. No circumstance or person can deflate it.

### Something to Do
Write down the names of those who could use your joy, your help, or your prayers today. Remember them during this week before Christmas. Drop them a card and let them know you're lifting them up through prayer.

### Something to Say
*Dear Lord, you are my joy. Today. Forever. Amen.*

## Thursday of the Fourth Week

*"The Mighty One has done great things for me."* Luke 1:49

# Never Give Up on Your Dream

Some people have a clear sense of their own destiny. Fictional character Simon Birch, from the movie of the same name, is one who believes he was put on Earth as "God's instrument," and he's gonna be a hero—although he's not sure how. He's quick to remind everyone that "God made me the way I am for a reason," and "God has a dream for everyone."

Do you remember when you were a kid? Life seemed so full of hope, didn't it? It can still be that way if we hold on to our dreams and never let them go. When I say dreams I mean the desires, hopes, and wishes that are deep within our hearts, waiting to be followed. No matter what our age or condition, there are still untapped possibilities within us and new dreams waiting to be born.

As we reach for our dreams we'll run into dream blockers who ridicule, sabotage, and discount any dream with detour comments: "You don't have what it takes; forget about it." "Stop kidding yourself. You're not smart enough." "

Let's remain dream makers with a passion for dreaming. To reach our dreams, we dream makers must build a special three-rung ladder. The first rung is determination, the second is dedication, and the third is attitude. When we give the best we have, when we refuse to be stopped by the obstacles in our way, when we do what must be done, we'll get what we deserve—a full, rich life that's like no other.

**Something to Do**
Schedule a family movie night. Rent the movie *Simon Birch* (Buena Vista, 1998) and watch it together. Afterwards, share your dreams with each other.

**Something to Say**
*Dear Lord, I believe you have big dreams for me. I'm determined to reach them. Amen.*

## Friday of the Fourth Week

*"He will be called John. But no one has this name."* Luke 1:60–61

# Embrace Change

Two things are certain in life: death and change. One is an end, the other a beginning. Change is life. Without change there would be no growth, no understanding, and no surprises. It's natural for us, yet we fear it and resist it more than any other aspect of life.

Elizabeth and Zechariah made a big break from tradition by naming their child John. This change prompted others to remark, "John? None of your relatives has this name." But they held firm and repeated, "His name is John."

Change happens when we've resisted changing our lifestyle or ignored our health and serious medical issues surface. Or when we take the people in our lives for granted and we're told, "I'm lonely. I'm leaving." But it doesn't have to come only as a result of realizing we are within one inch of losing our health or our family. It should come when we wake up to the multiple opportunities life holds before us. These opportunities enable us to grow while eliminating the routines that leave us trapped in dull, unhealthy, and stagnant lives.

Of course anything new, untested, and uncertain causes anxiety. But change has the power to uplift, heal, stimulate, open new doors, bring fresh experiences, and create excitement in life. When we embrace change, we'll discover that change is the greatest vehicle for achieving happiness and growth.

### Something to Do

Think back to a time when you experienced a change, but resisted. What happened once you embraced change? By remembering that changes improved your life in the past, you'll approach each new change with anticipation.

### Something to Say

*Dear Lord, I look back and say, "I'm glad I changed habits and behaviors. My life is so much better." Amen.*

## Saturday of the Fourth Week

*Give the people knowledge of salvation through the forgiveness of their sins.* Luke 1:77

# It's So Hard to Let Go

"She'll not live a day," a physician told the nurse. Concerned, the nurse befriended the dying woman, and in a few hours won her confidence. The old woman said sorrowfully, "I traveled all the way from California by myself, stopping at every city of importance between San Francisco and Boston. In each city I visit just two places: the police station and the hospital. You see, my son ran away from home and I have no idea where he is. I've got to find him."

The mother's eyes flashed a ray of hope as she added, "Someday he may even come into this hospital. If he does, please promise me you'll tell him his two best friends never gave up on him." Bending over the dying woman, the nurse softly whispered, "Tell me the names of those two friends so I can tell your son, if I ever see him." With tear-filled eyes the mother responded, "Tell him those two friends are Jesus and me." She then closed her eyes and died.

One of the hardest things we must do is to let go of something from the past. We can be our own harshest judges and chief tormentors, filled with guilt and regret over the choices we have made.

Jesus is not a wound opener, but a wound mender. Jesus knows that harboring resentment, holding a grudge, and rerunning the same hatred over and over only hurts us. We simply need to ask Jesus to help us forget the past, move on, and stop wasting valuable energy on anger, resentment, and revenge. After all, forgiveness really means to give it up for ourselves—not for the other.

**Something to Do**
Write a letter to Jesus expressing your thanks for his forgiveness.

**Something to Say**
*Dear Lord, you have forgiven me, you are forgiving me, and you will always forgive me. Thank you. Amen.*

## Christmas Day

*"When they saw this they made known the message told to them about this child."* Luke 2:17

# Christmas Spoken Here

I once saw a small sign in the corner of a beautiful Christmas shop that read: "Christmas Spoken Here." Would you agree that we need to speak and hear these words all year? The themes from three holiday movies can help connect us with the message of Christmas, and help keep it fresh 365 days a year.

In *A Christmas Carol*, one crippled boy, Tiny Tim, turns out to be the primary motivator for changing Mr. Scrooge into a steward of the good news. Consider making at least one of the Scrooges in your life your project for the year. All you need to soften their hearts is a positive attitude, a smile, and selfless love.

*How the Grinch Stole Christmas* carries a similar message. The Grinch's heart grew and he opened himself up to love. By responding to Scrooges with kind gestures, we may help sweeten the sourest humbug person.

*It's a Wonderful Life* shows us that, although George may not be financially secure after the angel gets his wings, he has what matters most: his wife and children's love and the richness of many friendships. Christmas is difficult for the lonely and the rejected. Pick someone who's a shut-in, in a nursing home, or whose grief is recent, and do something special for them on the twenty-fifth of each month.

Make Christmas one long, extended gift of ourselves to others.

**Something to Do**
Give one of the holiday movies to some of those who have everything. Better yet, invite them over to watch it, and discuss how it speaks Christmas all year. Then give it to them.

**Something to Say**
*Dear Lord, when I give someone the gift of myself, it never has to be returned after Christmas. Amen.*